WHISPERS OF THE SOUL

Inspired Texts, Poems and Guidance

ELIANE LEGAY-CLARKE

ISBN   978-1-80049-890-7

First Published 2021

© 2021 Eliane Legay-Clarke

DEDICATION

This book is dedicated with deep Gratitude to the Elder Brothers,
The Masters of the Great Brotherhood of Light.
To all Great Beings who have inspired these pages, to my
beloved students and friends
And to the Angel of the Presence, the I AM.

QUOTES

Everything awaits its time,
neither the rose blooms before its time,
nor the sun rises before its time,
wait, what is yours will come to you.

Hz. Celaleddin Mevlana RUMI

One must manifest discipline of spirit; without it one cannot
become free.
To the slave discipline of spirit will be a prison;
To the liberated one it will be a wondrous healing garden...

... He who has envisioned evolution will approach it carefully,
joyously brushing away the dust on the path.
Most important there will be no fear in him.
And rejecting the unnecessary he will acquire simplicity.
It is easy to understand that the realisation of evolution is
always beautiful.

Leaves of Morya's Garden Book Two: Illumination
1925, page 8 - Agni Yoga Society

GRATITUDE

My warmest thanks go to my dearest friend, Kylie Smith, a flower fairy of Oz, to whom I am indebted for the incredible work of creating, from start to finish, the book you have between your hands, arranging the design, fonts, presentation, cover illustration, etc.

Gratitude to my dear sister Lisa Stein for her foreword, to Michael Hawkins for his eagle eye in editing, and all those who have encouraged me on this path of Light.

It was a pure endearment for poetry and the music of words which have led my dearest friends and students to push me to persevere in publishing this work of Love.

My deepest gratitude to the Great Beings who have inspired these pages and guided me in the meanders of the source of words creating with them the pure guidance of their Light.

INTRODUCTION

From the Source of Inspiration...

In the sacred and secret universe of my inner life a window has opened to the voice of my soul. The warmth of the golden sun of my deep meditations has been inspirited in the labyrinth of exalted words of love emerging one by one in a celestial symphony.

In an instant the inspiration forced open the door of my inner silences and scattered its spiritual litanies as stardust in a winter sky.

The Word sprang forth like sap from its sheath of silence and was flushed with Love. So my quill began to run across the blank page filling it with its winged and graceful notes of inspiration. A celestial voice commanded my being to center in an incandescent beam and the words, between two states of birth, began to dance on my bare page.

WHY THIS BOOK?

For many their spiritual life is felt like a hesitation between understanding and confusion. For those on the probationary path, aspirants or disciples, this book can offer some inspiration in the maze of deep meanings they are not familiar with.

A few years ago, in group meditation, whilst focusing on inspirational texts and visualisations, I was inspired to write some guidances, often poetic, lofty sometimes, profound in their meaning and offering a soothing Light to the heart in our quest for Truth. They often had a deep effect on those present and more precisely offered them the exact inner inspiration they needed. As we are unique in our light and soul, our response to this type of stimuli may vary greatly. Sincere seekers on a spiritual journey are often quite receptive to some guidance, as it will help them persevere in their aspirations - even if this guidance earnestly urges the reader.

In my humble abode I received these meaningful communications-poems-messages from the Great Beings we regard as the Holy Brothers of our Souls, the magnificent riders of the Cosmic Oceans of Love, and more modestly inspired from my Soul, the Angel of the Presence.

I kept these inspired writings and poems in the bosom of my heart for far too long and realised that they must serve others on a spiritual journey in their very modest way of expression instead of sleeping aimlessly in the drawers of my desk...

It is those inspired writings I am presenting you today, inlaid with the jewels of the language of Love and bathing in the Light of our Spiritual Hierarchy.

I sincerely wish that they will serve you well and show you these alternative thoughts which lead to concrete actions. They will guide those thoughts impregnated with too much astral energy and will bring Light where you had darkness, a sense of purpose instead of erratic wondering, remove doubt and instability of the mind creating a new clarity.

At first whilst reading one may be perplexed, however after reading again you may realise the closeness of your own understanding.

In the following poem you may discover the guidance inlaid in Love and a sense of elevation of thought:

The Devic Lord blew His fire in the heart of man;
Sing the song of His heart before sunrise.
The Divine Mother sings in the heart of woman
and both songs bring the power of Love to rise.
Before the dawn of the East
The river of Love will cross the valley of Light.
The armies of Knights will chase the Beast
and the song of the children of God will resound right.
Anchor the destiny of those We love.
Fill to the brim the garden of their soul.
With our flags and banners We shall rise above
and pour over you the Chalice of Peace, the Holy Light of Love.

OM!   OM!

Keep reading through the pages at different times. Open a page at random. Let the sounds of the words impregnate the meanders of your mind. Divine help might await you at the corner of your Path. Some poems are not straightforward and need meditative time to comprehend their true meaning. Some are for "advanced disciples" and some for "probationers". Each one offers you their secret music hidden in the delicate flow of their words.

In the fold of a book resides the noble purpose of its existence. May you discover its intent. I have been pursuing the idea of serving - albeit very humbly - those on the Path of Light. They secretly wish with Love in their heart and the radiant Light of their soul to rise towards Shambhala and Christ, the World Teacher, at the heart of the Hierarchy.

If this book helps just one step, it will have accomplished its mission.

So be it.

Note: With the exception of a few texts, these poems-communications do not use the first person, the I, as I am only a quill and a hand with an open heart and a listening soul. Perhaps, Divine Inspiration is in the making...

FOREWORD

Let these magical words float off the pages to uplift you. Just as the Ancient Mysteries are often coded so that they will only make sense to those who are ready, so too will this poetry come to life in the eyes of the true disciple or initiate.

This poetry, written by my sister, Eliane, a fellow initiate on the path, represents to me the essence of Eliane's spirit. This journey is always challenging, and Eliane has found a way to bring a joie de vivre to light her way. She brings this same energy to this book of poetry, which she shares with us as her own gift to humanity.

It has been an honour for me to be asked to do this foreword for such enchanting work. Eliane has indeed put her heart and soul into this project of love, which is perhaps lifetimes in the making. Let the music of the words on these pages fill your heart and linger in the back of your mind to inspire you with light and love.

Lisa Stein

Important point on presentation of the text

Ahead of possible criticism, I would like to make some comments about the words written with capital letters. Those words belong to the essence of their definition and they are used in their pure sense, in their music and intrinsic nature such as: Light, Beauty, Harmony, Love, Joy, Spirit, Mother of the World and many others. As these texts were inspired by Masters, Great Beings, in which often They urge earnestly the reader, capital letters have been used in respect for Them, such as Our, They, Them, We, etc.

I sincerely hope it won't disturb your reading whilst you will appreciate the meaning of these inspired poems and guidance.

Divine is the ardent Law of Love
It perfumes the heart and the soul.
Light will always shine from above
Use it with Wisdom as a divine tool.

In the gardens of your tomorrows
Will thrive the exquisite beauty of the rose
As the song of your soul ascends without sorrow
your devotion to the Hierarchy swiftly arose.

Quieten, quieten, quieten.
Our voice is as soft as honey.
Follow Me. Our path is steep,
but the mountains are welcoming.
Rise from the ordinary.
Silence is your best friend,
And the bird songs are joy.
The rainbows will enliven the skies.
Purity has a rich glow.
It will glow in your sky.

War is in the hearts and minds of men.
The unsettled legions are now gathering.
Distortion and deceit are the new omen
Having lost their shepherd the sheep are fearing.

Your mandala is the way to reach Us with a horn.
Its sound will call the flocks of Shambhala.
At sunrise, a new star will have to be born.
Its light will brighten the kingdom of the Deva.

The blazing and ardent crests of the mountains
Will be transformed under the swords of Light.
Our banners will reveal the path to Our fountains
And lead you to wash the remains of your plight.

The West has defected the territory.
Purity has its gates and virtues.
In the corridors of life We present opportunities.
The cohesion of all Initiates is Our banner of Joy.
In the intensity of all battles and fights
Our song will resonate in the four corners.
Intensify your silence and meditations.
The power of Our messages will increase
and your hearts will bleed with Love.
Learn the way of profound calmness
and the Spirit of the Mother will inhabit your soul.

The divine hours have their rhythm.
Do not leave a blank page.
The book needs to be written
The flow of Joy will be infused with it.

Remit your doubts in the cradle of Love
and the amber mornings will become Truth.
Our Presence is becoming familiar
in the deep silences of dawn.
Your Love song will raise as a promise amidst the fights.
Do not be afraid of combats.
There are fruits which need to ripen.

If one has held the Seven between his hands
the Ten should be borne in the mandala.
The Eight has the grace of a petal
And the Nine holds the secret of the book.
If Two has a bonnet, then the Lord
will ascend on the mount of Orion.
Beware of the strength of the One
as it always leads to the multiple.
Beloved, learn to count the steps
on the stairs of My heart.
Not one should be missed.
The numbers have their own music
which resonates in the cosmic depths.

OM!

In the spring morning of your awakening,
the effusive Love of the Mother is hatching seeds of Light.
Her silky devas, filled to the brim with the new dawning,
guard and lead their form to express perfection and might.
In His sacred heart of compassion Christ
raises your consciousness
to the pure field of giving and service, initiation and oneness.

Ô Disciples! Hearken the sound of Our benevolence
and the song of the dove.
In the cradle of Shambhala, the golden age is being born.
Fill your heart with the sunrise of Rebirth and your words
with the honey of Love.
In the antechamber of Om, Wisdom is showing
its future splendour.

O Children of God
Brothers and Sisters of mine,

The sword has revealed the Might.
Each of your hearts is anchored in its blade.
Do not throw away the past as it has shaped your future.
But the page is open in the book of the Twelve and you will
write the next chapter of the Hierarchy of Light.
Hearken the song of the dove.
Beyond the towers is the song of Purity and Wisdom.
I call you by your name, the only one We know.
In the intensity of now the colours of peace are like diamonds
on the crown of Our divine Brother.
Christ overshadows this moment in the immensity
of the plain.
His wings covering the book of Humanity and the
seven solar systems.
May the sisters lead the pace of charity and compassion.
The feminine contains all. The Love of God pours His
golden nectar into your wombs of Light.
In face of adversity your hands will hold the sword
and use it with the song of the scriptures.
Your lips are sealed on the purpose and only your hearts
will speak the language of Shambhala.
In chaos the germ of the future can grow strong and healthy.
May Peace be upon you!

OM!   OM!   OM!

The devas dance with the energy of Love
weaving the lace of unity in the realm of life.
Their veils protect the wings of the dove
and their songs ascend amidst the towers of Might.
Love has dressed the triangle of dawn
And removed the weight of all inequity.
In the sequence of evolutionary dawnings
Love in truth and goodness will be revived in serenity.
Empower your hearts and spirit, My Beloved!
Your tomorrows will face the ascent of your unity.
With your swords of Light and your flaming hearts
your battles are the landscape of Our Shambhalic Might.

OM!

The Instructor has prepared the verses of Destiny.
In the flight of days Hope has put its train.
The Diamond scintillates even in the heart of the night.
The pearls of Wisdom adorn the morning stars.
The way of the Heart is lined with their radiance.

The paths of the Universe are blanketed with snow.
The doors of Faith are bathing in the Light.
In the scarlet of the battle,
Our banner will be seen from each wing of the horizon.
Blue will be the conqueror
and the rainbow shall enlighten the way to Our Mansion.
Teach the Joy of the Future!
Teach the Path of Light!
Weapons of war will have only one creed.

Imperial are My ways
Sweet is My voice.
Hearken the sounds of disarray
Love, pray and rejoice.

Hearken the salve of victory
Wear the mantle of Joy.
In your bundle of unity
A star is being born.

The Mother sits on the throne of Destiny
Her armies fill the sky with their blue indigo.
In Her heart She holds Mercy,
Her feet firmly on the ocean of old.

Rise from the cinders of the past.
The Sun is glorious in the eyes of the erudite.
Love is dressed in the east.
His sunrise beams on the horizon.
Write with words that love and shine.
Sing the deva song of the Awakening.
Haste! Haste, the gates are open
to rebirth and chanting.

Colours of Light
Colours of Love
Consciousness is bright
and Light is your Love.
Your group weaves
the mandala of eternity.
Be ready for Our tomorrows
for darkness, the future is bleak.
Dragons and Unicorns in many rows
head for victory of the Light.
High in the sky your swords
shine in the rebirth of Might.
Your colours weave the mantle of dawn...

The dove of the future
flies above the abyss.
Firm are the hands of the Beloved.
Strong are the voices of conquest.
War is coming from the West
Ready you are in your colourful shine.
Your hearts united
on the altar of Love
Our knights you are
under Our banner of Light.
The purple river brimming with red
is engulfed in the ocean of blue.
The Mother pours the water of Purity
above the canyon of desolation.

Pray beloved Ones; Time is of the essence!
Raise your consciousness and see dawn
on the horizon of Hope.
Live only for the Future!
Grace inhabits your souls.

In the garden of your heart there is a rose.
Each of its petals belongs to Shambhala.
You have not lost one.
All petals will display their Grace as Love is expressing
its true nature within you.
Red is the colour of your strength and will.
Red is the colour of action.
Remember the devas.

The unicorn has walked above
the abyss of your incertitudes.
Firm your grip on the path of Love.
The Kingdom of Shambhala
welcomes your gratitude.
Rise above all vicissitudes
and you should be freed of Karma.
The I has integrated the whole.
Devotion is required.

The colourful Chohans
have passed the bridge of Destiny.
Swords of Light in their hands,
Their powerful song of Love and unity
echoing around the Shambhalic lands.
In a field of lilies
Our steeds of Light march
and blow the steam of Love.
The Mother of the World
rides Her white dove
and commands the Deva army.
She is counting Her beads,
Her hair floating like a sea.
The Moon and the Sun have copulated.
Lord Sirius is on His way!

Beauty in our midst
is sowing the seeds of Love.
Scatter away the schism
and rise to My abode.

The one and two
Are reunited to the seven
as the ten unfolds its flower
Perfection is achieved then.

Gold is the Light of the One
but he is also the seven.
All petals are one
at the threshold of Heaven.

The golden guardian of the east
has entered His cycle of Love;
He is weaving the bridge above the abyss
anchoring the magic of the dove.

The seventh has laid His eggs in your nest.
From one to seven, the journey of beauty has
graced your heart.
Remember the steps that lead to the Eye.
Consciousness ascends with will and Love.
In each of your heart, We sow Our own seeds,
Caring for your garden.
The sounds of your colours are becoming the
divine symphony We love to hear.
Hearken! Hearken, Brothers and Sisters of mine.
In the grave hour brewing is the seed of the
beauty of tomorrow.
Gather your strength and Love, the Hierarchy needs
your pure heart and dedication.
The cosmic devas are prepared for your journey.
Never forget Sirius.
The alchemy of His Heart has transformed your destiny
(as a Group).
The Verb has to be received and pronounced.
Prepare your steeds of glory.
Their canter will resonate on the path to Shambhala.

The bridge has been set alight.
The two worlds will be One.
In the room of the future
I will give you Teachings.
Bear high the flag of the Hierarchy.
We, Masters, have no time for petty things.
The entire world is one step in the future.
Everything is planned.

Knowledge is a seal which needs to be broken
so as to know the world beyond.
Our great Family has its own wheels.
Shambhala is the Triangle and the Eye,
the pentagram and the hexagram.
Each tip of each triangle has its own manifestation,
its wheels and its colours.
We overshadow your progress.
Pure is the heart of the true learner.
The Seven always accompanies the One.

The wheels of life are like resplendent jewels.
Over the rainbow the sounds will be heard.
Listen to these sounds.
They lead to your path and to the temple.
The Sun will have to rise three times
before its light will shine on the house.
A radiant halo guides your thoughts and dreams.
Blue, bright and gold is tomorrow for the one who dares.
Shambhala is hovering.
The dark clouds veil Our voice.
Keep rising!

The eastern wind brings the breath of ignorance.
The sacred hour has been heard by the purest of hearts
Raise your swords of Light, Brothers and Sisters.
Follow the path of stones and mud amidst the songs
of Shambhala.
Our great devas have traced the road to Victory.
Listen to their songs in the garden of your heart.

Doubt is your worst enemy.

The blood of faith runs in the veins of silence.
Our voice is soft but is heard throughout the canopy of stars.
Pacify your hearts and souls. Sing the flamed song of Unity.
We are startled by the assault but it gives us the joy of seeing
the three and the seven on their steeds.

In the nights and dawns, We draw the curtain of Truth.
Our knights wear the cross and the star.
West sinks in the sunset of lies.
The red crescent basking in the moonlight,
Clouds whisper the words of plight.
O sisters of Mine, bring reason into the hearts of mankind.
We are your flame, your heart and your mast.
Eons flow under the bridge of becoming.
Green will radiate but the blue will reign with the
red as the guide.

Children of the Earth,
My Being is your Being.
We are One.
I am ever changing.
I am the Eternal Presence.
Raise your consciousness
you will see more and more
in your eye's mind.
We are not coming to you.
Raise your consciousness
and thus We reveal Our Presence.
Each solar system has its own Being.
Within My Being
I have engulfed the Milky Way.
Multiple are My worlds
but unique is My Mind.
The Earth is a cell in My body.
My divine knights are on Earth
and you are the essence of their swords.
Love is the matter of your soul.
Your path is made of Love.
Rise above. Rise! Rise! Rise!
Light! Light! Light!
I Am. I Am. I Am
the Ancient of Days.

Steeds of fire, We are
Fire of your hearts.
Fire of your soul, We are
and a fire very smart:
It blows the seven colours
of the temple of Love.
Pillars of the temple, We are
as true Knowledge and Wisdom.
Our thundering ways, We are,
For your becoming out of the bosom.
Our chest contains the fountain of Om,
But AUM is everywhere.
The gate is open to the pure and fair.
The sound bounces on your fence of Love.
Steeds of fire We are, in the air.
Blessed we are by the Masters of Love.

Your third eye is asleep under the canopy of illusions.
Only the Master can remove its veil.
Sound and colour are one in the temple of consciousness.
In the cradle of Love, the tension has emerged.
Like the chord of the violin, it vibrates in resonance with
your soul.
Souls are linked to each other in the web of your mandala.
All Masters observe your web of Light and thus
know your wisdom, know your sound.
Approach sound like a warrior:
In its beauty reposes its power.

A leaf has landed on the water of Love.
The Verb has left its divine print in it.
The sound of the Verb is hovering above,
The presence of the Father, and the Mother,
swirling into it.

Quanta of thoughts have gathered on the divine leaf.
Let their melody be released in the vacuum of the future.
On the bridge of Hope leaves are scattered by the thief;
But the children of Love patiently rebuild the structure.

Brothers and Sisters of Love
Open your hearts to the divine melody.
In your modest but bright abode
Our steeds of fire work tirelessly.

Peace be upon you.
Shambhala is your aim
and the Hierarchy your family.

These are 9 short sentences coming from different Beings.

The gate of the east has opened its golden door on the valley of Hope.

Only those with pure hearts will follow its course.

The link of Love has been sealed with the eye of the north.

The canter of Our steeds will be heard between each of your thoughts.

The sword of Christ shines above your temple.

Its power will be felt in the coming era.

The white Dragon is guarding its secret in the vault of Shambhala.

The Teacher holds the key and its ribbons.

Our great Lord is awakened and His tongue speaks Truth.

Truth and Wisdom dance with Love.
Their triplicity is accomplished in the heart of the initiate.
Intelligence brings the depth of knowledge needed for
the initiation.
The ebb and flow of the three emphasizes the One.
In the weaving of eons, the sounds of their music have
draped the house of virtues.
Disciples, meditate on the three to understand the two.
Then the one will appear.
Unity is your banner weaved in Love.
The arrows of will bring the intensity of Light on the
landscape of Love.
Beauty resides in the combination of the three and its
heart reveals Our Love.
Continue your path of initiation with Our Divine Love
in your heart.
Truth should reveal itself in your flaming mind.

To Groups...

The divine energy of Love has spread its wings in the
heart of your temple.
Each of you is a ring in the chain of the cradle of initiations.
Focus on the intensity of Light you can emit as we tie loops
between each soul revealing a geometry known in Shambhala.
Thread the path of your future with strength like a mast
securing the boat of Destiny.
Ardent is your courage and soothing is your compassion for
these difficult planetary times.
We have prepared all maps for guidance and revelation.
Combats are your daily routines as they reinforce your will
to conquer Love and for Love.
The lace of your nadis is enlivened by your purity of intent
and give your monad the field on which We impress
Our colourful thoughts.
The diamonds of your minds have been cleansed
and their shining splendour allow messages to be manifested.
Hearken, soldiers of Love!
Even in the worst of attack We are by your side.
Never again should you feel the isolation of solitude.
The red is copulating with the blue thus your hearts are
gilded with the empowerment of actions.
In the regal room of Shambhala We hold your souls between
Our hands and together they are the Dove of Peace.

Twelve is the number of completion for those involved.
Take care of your petals as they are the jewels of your soul.
Indigo blue is your laser beam of Love.
Only when the true heart is awakened can you manifest its
colour and use it for Service.
The lower heart is only preparatory and takes many lives
to surpass.
Brothers and Sisters of Mine,
the indigo blue colour helps most of you to manifest the red.
We add the silver and golden hues of the Shambhalic mandala
for empowering your temple.

There is only transformation, transmutation.
Nothing disappears.
Everything evolves in another state of consciousness.
The robes should be worn in their full colour.
From the microscopic to higher beings such as planets
and systems,
every living being helps others to evolve, to grow.
There is a multiplicity of minds in one Avatar so to
encompass all evolution
in His system (solar or planetary).
The mandala is the representation of a complex entity with a
mind made of many a soul.
Love is a complex concept made of a multitude of attributes.
The power of Love resides in the use of the purest of
each attribute.
The future holds a truth you cannot yet imagine but your
soul knows.
Your struggles will be rewarded in ribbons of Light.
Remember the Star of the east and the King of the north.
The Divine Mother is empowering each of you with the
diamonds of Her true nature.

To Groups...

Have the courage to grow and dream.
Have the will to glow and shine.
Take the opportunity to serve and give.
Take the hands of the Masters with your heart.
Brave tempests and storms in the midst of peace.
Brave all changes that are required.

Hearken, Sisters and Brothers!
The foundations of your temple are sound.
Its walls built with the cement of your Unity.
The roof, dome and towers are filled with your Light.
Your united hearts are its pure Love and strength.

Unite! Unite! at all times!
Bear the vicissitudes with a smile
and share your joy and victories!
Be One in the midst of the battle
in the same way as the Sirian people are One:
their shine and beauty are entrusted in your sword.

Beware of counterfeits and jealousy!
Beware of those who speak in Our name!
Rise, rise above all the malevolence of intents.
Raise, raise your divine consciousness
and merge with Our own.
The diamond of Our heart embraces yours.

OM!

To Groups...

The horses of fire have hastened their canter.
The song of Shambhala is resonating in the fields of dawn.
Sing in unison as your voices are the mirror of the OM.
The Star shall shine above your temple carrying the name of
the Son in its centre.
The Teacher has spelled out Our Will and Our Love.
Take a bath of this vivifying energy as the Lord spoke
through His voice.
Our decision should be followed to the letter. Your unity is
dear to us and vital.
Bear the coming events with courage.
Your love will be tested as the battle is raging in the
minds of men.
Judgment is also your enemy.
Remember it takes a lot of effort to surmount temptations.
Through your hands, see Our hands.
Through your hearts, see Our hearts.
The steps of Our temple of Light shine before your soul.

OM!

The fire within is the drive and the tension.
Without fire Our will cannot be fulfilled.
Your unified hearts are your burning fire.
Around Our fire, Our Love, gather united!
Remember: you are part of the book.

Prepare your vessels for the great sea,
The wind of the north shall bring you to the portal.
There, the deva Lords sing the song of the veil.
Then, the Sun will shine above the flotilla.
Ignite the fire of Truth, of Love and of Light.
We shall keep your abode under the fire of Our hearts.

OM!   OM!   OM!

Joy is the way, joy is the song
Garner your heart with joy and Love
as it is Our mantra, Our song
The unique voice of the dove.

Sing the song that sings
Say the word that transforms
Wisdom adorns all beginnings
and Love lies in all cosmic forms.

Stanza for the Initiate

Be the transformer
Practise silence
Meditation deepens your listening
Be aware of Our presence at all time
Yield more. Battle less.
In the silence of dawn
your spirit soars to the Sun.
Be prepared for the task ahead.
With your Love as your Light,
your acts of will have weight.
Reveal the glory of God in the hour of thirst.
Raise your consciousness to Our OM.
Be the sound We want to hear.
Your time has come to express Our will
as Our steeds of fire are facing the east.
Do not lure the past, its pastures have weeds.
The fields of the future have flowers.
Hurry to cleanse your robe.
Cultivate Truth.
Remember: "sacrifice is first of all a possibility"
said our Brother Morya.
We give possibilities.
Learn about sacrifice the way the world sacrifices itself.
Heighten your gaze!
Blow the cosmic Rays of Love.
Raise your sword of Light
to the Glory of the Lord Christ!
to the Glory of the Lord Buddha!
The unlimited possibilities of Our care
will illuminate your path.
Dare to act. Dare to love the unlovable.
Dare to stand for Truth.
There are battles and battles.
Discriminate the one you want to win!
Then, the mantle of Peace shall fall on your shoulders.

May the ineffable thoughts of Our Heart inspire you!

OM!   OM!   OM!

Light is the call
Light is the way.
There is no bliss without Light
There is no way without Love.
There is turmoil beneath your temple
Emotions are your setback
Free them with the sound.
Free them with the Light,
the river of gold bonding its petals.

Many a soul is waiting your flight
Their wings closed in the silence of the heart
Reveal your wings to the world
if you want it to learn Our way of Light.

The Father has spoken to the Son.
The sons of the Son stood in silence.
The Mother of the World raised her finger
and the river of Light gushed out of the mountain top.
The blue sisters speak the tongue of the stars
and Cassiopeia reveals Her splendour.
Elevate your heart to the heavens
Bring Humanity to the field of the Mother.
The songs of the enlightened One
resonate in the heart of the true initiate.

To me.. and all on the Path of Light.

An expanded consciousness has emerged
like a sun upon the field of Mind.
The conquering unity has blossomed
leaving the healed past behind.

Open the door of your heart centre
and ascend the towers of Knowledge,
riding on a steed of Light at a canter.
Soon, you will reach the hut of the Sage.

Fiery strength is needed in the discourse of Wisdom.

Words are the arrows of the initiate
but the words of the Father are the shield.
Sacrifice the words for the heart and yield
as silence has filled the Lord's dictate.

The golden gate is flooded with Light
waiting for the heart to come to the threshold.
Hear the sound of the river of Light,
the new deva Queen should reveal Her crown.

OM!

To Ruth...

Three times I sent the Light around your form
Three times I sung the song around your heart
Three times I lift the veil upon your mind
Three times I revealed three shields of Self.

Be aware of the fragility of form
Strengthen your field of Love
Meditate upon My heart and head
My field of thoughts will protect your Light.

Give full access to your soul
Raise above the destructors of Might
and enter the purity of the cauldron of fire.

Three times we send Our Om and Hum.
Three times We raise upon your heart.

OM!   OM!   OM!

To Anastassiya...

Blessed is the one with the velvet dress
Blessed is her lineage and descendants.
In the kingdom of Tibet she lived.
Her ladder was steep.
Her courtyard filled with incense.

Clouds came from the east
and she had to flee and hide.
In a cave she meditated for aeons
where her body rose to the Light.

Repa she wore on the peak of the mountain
and she became the sound and the music of Om.
In the river of consciousness, she has to renew her vows
The essence of Love is her book to write.
The wings of the dove overshadows her life.

Prayer for those who Love...

Dear Lord,

Help us to raise above the ocean of the personality
Give us the strength to achieve all our endeavours
Throw away our lacks and feebleness in search of Verity
Bring us the fundamental Truth for our soul to savour.

Our united hearts create the mandala of Your Divinity
The depth of our manifested rays is anchored in their
true colours.
Our creative Minds adorn the sky above,
between now and Infinity
The pure flower of our soul swirls its scent around,
healing all horrors.

We ride firmly our steeds of Light wearing the white robe
of the Knights.
Around the lake of initiations our common jewel float
with Serenity.
We have vowed to reveal Your incandescent face.
We have vowed to wear the colours of Your Divine Love.
On the way to the bridge of dawn, we race,
ready for the battle, our bright swords raised high above.

Dear Lord, Humility and Joy are part of our dutiful life
Service is the unique task we perpetuate amidst Humanity
Ready are our hearts to survive all wounds and strife
We bow to Your Grace and Love in the morning of Infinity.

OM!   OM!   OM!

Imperative is the ascent of Self
Humble is the pursuit of power
Inexhaustible is the thirst for Knowledge
Precious is the pilgrimage of the sower

The book is whispering the Truth
The altar is on the mountain top
The Dakinis dance on the sound of the flute
their bare feet warming the consecrated rock.

Leave your bag on the threshold of Our Home
Sing the song of the white robes
Bathe your eyes in the mist of dawn
Rest upon the diamond river of Love.

The Cross still stands at the crossroad of initiation
Its arms wide open towards the heart of God.
The pillar of the colours of the rays dressed as revelation,
Upon the mount of tests and sacrifices, it shows its abode.

To Groups..

Initiates of My heart!
Guide those lost in the fields of illusions
Pray for the forbearance of the aspirants
Greet the Devas in grand attire with communion
Love the pilgrim on his path leading up to the Presence.

Radiate the unfailing faith of the Beloved
Forgive the blind, the dumb and the deaf of heart
Share the abundance of the table of the provided
Hearken the instructor guiding your souls forward!

The Sirian Lord has crossed the bridge of Destiny
You are being prepared for the brightest of stars
Wisdom stepping over the radiant rainbow of Infinity
Hearken the song of Love in Our flaming hearts.

OM!   OM!   OM!

We are at the threshold of a moment.
Our Light is strong at the edge of war.
Peace is the focus of Our actions and prayers.
We affirm Our complete dedication to the Lords.
Sanctify your thoughts and deeds.
Keep your heart like a flaming sword,
its radiance shall transform rage into Love.
The power of Love wins always over hatred.
The alchemy of a flaming heart ignites the indifferent
and the fearful,
raising the desire for Service and Dedication.

Steps have to be made very carefully.
Towards the north is the path of initiation.
Honour the heart and Buddhi
Strengthen Truth for the sake of all nations.

If our twenty meet your seven
Nine times the song of Shambhala will be heard.
In the corridor of deceit some are like brethren
Pay heed to the true song of the bird.

All sisters should be one united in fire.
Their mantle ripples under the breeze of the east.
There is no time for mourning on the pyre
Only unity of heart and Love can beat the beast.

The youngest might reveal to be the oldest
Pearls of wisdom are between her hands.
With patience and virtue her necklace will brighten the west
Then the Deva Lords will bow and dance.

Halt the anguish of lack
Break the habit of worry
Bear the heat of our Light
Wear Our robe of Glory

The white hat has much power
but the green robe has to be worn
The golden eagle will fly to its lair
raising the Word that has to be sworn.

To Groups...

The lotus has appeared on the lake of birth.
Its scent impregnates the rays of Mind
and its petals are open to the flow of thirst.
Be watchful and keep purity as your friend.

The Lord is glad of your company,
His Eye fills the space of the garden.
His tongue speaks the sound of infinity
and His words bear the strength of the burden.

Hearken brothers and sisters of mine!
The swan has folded its two wings.
Above the lake of silence and rhyme
his long neck reposes in Our winds.

Brave the laboured effort of stillness.
In the midst of Our towers Our sound is loud.
Discern the music within selflessness
and enter into the note we sing aloud.

Soar above the reef of stress and ill,
giving more thoughts to your becoming.
Our shields are ready and Our lake still.
Our Blessings rest upon your yielding.

OM!

The symphony of the world has different scales.
Hearken the one no one can hear but your soul.
Silence is the music of the words of Love.
To form one note with many souls: this is a Sangha:
a work of unity in the cradle of the heart.
The power of the note will gush out like a fountain of youth
and give its sword to the right knights of Mind.
The sound is bound to the gathering of Light
and myriads of devic presences will obey to its thunder.
Hearken, hearken the voice of the Mother;
her song flaunts her army of Light.
In the garden of the soul We sing Our hymn of victory.
Gather the flowers in buds and the petals of the old
and create the bouquet of harmony and sound.
Affirm your path led by the scent of eternity
and pay heed to the Shambhalic sound.

OM!   OM!   OM!

The Devic Lord blew His fire in the heart of man;
Sing the song of His heart before sunrise.
The Divine Mother sings in the heart of woman
and both songs bring the power of Love to rise.
Before the dawn of the east
The river of Love will cross the valley of Light.
The armies of knights will chase the Beast
and the song of the children of God will resound right.
Anchor the destiny of those We love.
Fill to the brim the garden of their soul.
With our flags and banners We shall rise above
and pour over you the chalice of Peace, the Light of Love.

OM!   OM!   OM!

Addressed to me but also to all sisters..

Rise! Rise! Daughter of mine!
Bring your light close to Our Might!
Stay humble and brave but shine
as lure and war will be the closest sight.
Approach the bridge of all consolation
with the heart of a warrior and of a deva.
Tear apart all doubts and hesitation
as firm is your service to Shambhala.
The visions you hold are sacred and true.
Rest upon the mountain of silence
and they shall reveal their meaning through and through.
Your sangha and yourself are revealing Our Presence.
Look at the infinity of the Universe:
Our Brothers of Space wait for the awakening!
The finger of the Great Lord has fired those dispersed
and His Love cries above like a lightning.

OM!

Symbolic images are made true in face of your consciousness.
We send them from the Buddhic plane as archetypal ideas.
They are the future in becoming and their petals have
received the scent of Our Wisdom.
Pay heed to their meaning as it is the only way Hierarchy can
express its thoughts.
Scent, colours and sounds bear the mark of Our intent.
Ritualise your life more as a ritual is the gate through which
We enter.
It is a sacred geometry in four dimensions and more..
Mantras are the river of sound into which We pour Our Love.
The seven sisters have to form the mandala of Our names.
This will be the anchor of Our feet on Earth.

Think of Light not of darkness!
Think of Hope not of despair!
Work with your soul and her kindness.
Work like the eagles in their lair.

Ô Warriors! Defenders of Our Might!
Charge on the lords of the dark faces
Remember! Your swords are of Light
and your heart is the vessel of Faith.

Wherever you go, We are with you!
Whatever you say, your words are Ours.
Whatever your battle, We combat with you.
We guard you, even in the small hours!

Recognise Our call in each slice of time.
Hearken Our sound in the silent hours!
The trumpets of destiny echo your striving,
the manifestation of beauty is Ours!

In the ocean of cosmic Harmony
the waves of Love sway Our influence!
Stand firm on the boat of Hierarchy!
In Our very names, sow Our true Essence!

OM!   OM!   OM!

The Seven have conquered the Mind-Heart.
With the help of the One and Two
the Hierarchy will glow with a new chart.
Bow to the Eye and elevate your soul.
There is urgency in the now.
Bear in mind Our helping hand!
Faith and strength will be your bow,
the arrow will be sent on Our command.
Your unified rays forming the banner,
only Love will seduce all enemies.
Bring this Love-Light to the Divine Mother
and there, She will bless your strong unity.

OM!   OM!   OM!

The leaves of Wisdom are on the altar.
We are pleased with the labour of Love.
The momentum has to be chosen from afar
so that the pearls can be given from above.

Reach the power of time and dedication.
Persevere in all endeavours for Our House of Fire.
Only a ground well prepared in devotion
will give the reward of years on a pyre.

Raise your consciousness to the domain of OM.
Brave the winds of the north on the boat of peace.
Battles have to be won on the pier of Home
but your shields are adorned with the "fleur de lys"!

Bow to the One in this brave hour.
Silence is dense before the intensity of dawn.
Gather around the Shambhalic hour
as the waves of Our Love permeate your gown.

Don't leave the doors open to uncertainty.
Gather your strength! We urge you not to weaken!
At each breath gather your unity
as a gathered flock is stronger for heaven.

OM!   OM!   OM!

Like a flower the petals of your soul will unfold.
Hardship is a necessity to cleanse the past.
The depth of the lesson to learn are from the old.
Nothing destructive should arise on your mast.

The path of Love is lifted by the spirit of the Lord.
The essence of Our hearts permeate your deeds.
Hold firm the sword of Light above the Word
The pages of destiny are instilled in each deed.

Ô Sisters of Old! Stand high on your temple of dawn.
I repeat again: Unify your hearts and Mind.
Your combats are Our combats as Sirius rises.
Wear the colours of your soul ray before those blind.
Your mast of Light shall shine like a sunrise!

OM!   OM!   OM!

The blue of Love is uplifted by the red of Will.
The red of Will reinforces the blue and its influence.
They are both woven in the knot of cosmic Infinity.
When the power of Love is combined with the Will,
the radiance of deeds submerges their field
and this effulgence illumines the intricate lace of Love.
The red flowers awaken the strength of your motivation.
The blue flowers enhance calmness in your soul aura.
But keep the Green in thought as on its bridge
Mind is dancing.
The Divine Mother is the source and Her emerald glitters
in the clear atmic Light.

Mind extends its wings to the four quadrants.
The transient aspect of Self inhabits between.
Its rainbow is everchanging and ever evolving
Self is impermanence permanent.
Consciousness is linked to Self and
consciousness is everchanging.
Experiences reveal your plane of consciousness
thus increasing your perception of Self.
Love then can express itself on the bridge
as perceptions become more subtle and refined.
The marriage between Mind and consciousness
harbours the beauty of the cosmic Lord.
In the Sunyata[1] sea, consciousness is bathing in the
eternal Atom
Then the dharmakaya[2] way is purified in the well of Love.

1. Sunyata - (Sanskrit) *Śūnyatā* A void, vacuum, emptiness; the Boundless or Void. In mystical philosophy, especially Mahayana Buddhism, illusory being or existence, the emptiness of cosmic manifestation when compared with the nonmanifest reality.

2. Dharmakaya - It is that spiritual body or state of a high spiritual being in which the restricted sense of soulship and egoity has vanished into a universal (hierarchical) sense, and remains only in the seed, latent — if even so much. It is pure consciousness, pure bliss, pure intelligence, freed from all personalising thought.

From Athanor...

Our pristine innermost landscapes await your awakening.
The innerly glow of Our hearts permeates all planets
and systems
The Love of the Mother is Our guide and Our knowing.
We unite in an effulgent stream and pour the Light of
Our aim.

The transcendence of Earth is the ultimate goal
as Humanity needs to evolve faster.
Open your Mind to Our impulse and role
Streams of divine Light need to be anchored deeper.

To me...

O daughter of Mine,
The Mother has shown you Her stairs
and Her stars shine in the landscape of your soul.
Dress yourself with the mantle of Peace and persevere,
the purity of your heart is the land where We rule.
On the mountain top I am awaiting your step.
Carrying the weight of the cross of Love and Service,
We shall meet at the time of yielding and sunset.

OM!

To all Initiates...

The Sirian Lord has come under the Arch of Light.
The army of Good is empowered by the Presence.
Ô Initiates! Prepare to receive the sword of Might
as the colours of the banner reveals its essence.
The crucible of the Lord is filled to the brim
but the nectar of the words wait for Love.
Raise your consciousness to the world of the Seraphim
as your spirit soars to the threshold of Their abode.

The rigour of thinking encompasses Wisdom
The mathematical evolution of the old systems
still bear the fruits in the present genome
but the Verb is brighter within its Light stems.
The path of Love has to be travelled far.
The unity of your hearts symbolises Our Truth and Light
The Verb of the Ancient of Days has sprung afar
to reveal the starseed in the vein of Might.

Daughters of Our Hearts stand firm on the threshold of Birth
as We pour the wine of Christ in your Soul
The book of the Old will increase your thirst
and please the Mighty One, soothing His divine Rule.

The rays of Mind must all be awakened
The page of the future has already been turned.
Sharpen your listening. Avoid all burden.
We have dropped the parchment from the Enlightened.

When a spiritual gift has to be given,
it needs to be offered with Love and Wisdom.
The words and their sounds are made in heaven.
The colours they bear should reveal the Dome.

Serene is the path to Enlightenment.
Your sufferings are the petals of the flower.
Brave hardship aiming to achievement.
The fruits of initiation have ripened in the Higher.

In the heart of My Heart is a Flower;
The seven rays of Mind are its petals of Love.
The Father has written a note on ether
The Father's Heart is infused with the heart of the dove.

The Lord is riding on the mountain tongue
His banner has to be washed in a spring.
His steed of fire sings the primordial song
The Father's heart is bound to the Light of spring.

If your heart bleeds in the despair of dawn,
Drink the cup filled with the bijas of Love.
My Heart must drink the source of your bemoan
and raise your heart to the Mighty One above.

Before spring can blow its flowers in your heart
The bridge of the Beloved has to be constructed.
It should be sound and strong under its arch,
as Light shines forth and bright like a magnet.
Bring with you your dress of ritual and gathering.
Wear the ribbons of your initiate attire.
The Shambhalic Brothers wait for your diamond ring
In the name of the Father They will walk on fire.
Have your steeds ready in their full splendour.
Pettiness has no place under the flame of the Old.
The heart of the Heart has long awaited for this hour.
Be ready: the All Seeing-Eye might be bold.

OM!

The river of gold is flowing under the bridge of dawn.
Develop the courage to stand all alone.
On the path of initiation, the abyss is on each side
and only with your white steed you can ride.

Division does not always mean separation.
The starry lights are for those who can see.
The tongue of the Heart needs to speak in compassion
to bear fruits on the Tree of Life for all to see.

Rites and prayers occupy the heart
The four squares are entering the temple
The mandala of Light is a work of art
Add the colours that represent Our mantle.

Sacrifice is the only door to the new dawn
Love has many facets of Light
Its pearls shine on the seat of the throne
Yield initiates! Om is in the midst of Our Might.

My words are made of the triangle and the sphere.
You need to understand the triangle before reaching the sphere.
The weight of My words bear on Humanity
and bring about the Sun fire and its Beauty.
Remain still in the void of the unfoldment
as the nectar of My words needs to impregnate your Light.
Reveal Our Wisdom only to those who reach attainment
as they could be burned in the fire of our Might.
Rise before the Sun of Our House of Heart.
Pray for the awakening of your Heart-Mind.
May your desire of Love respond to the song of Our Heart
In the realm of Light, Our steeds are Our Mind.

The summer silver wings have to land on the field of horses
as they carry the banner of the Teachings of Old.
The mountains will wait two moons and some storms
to bear the fruits of our school of gold.
The old sage must wear his old robe and his hat;
this simple attire will suit the events of the awakening.
Solitude is the key as the road leads to a new domain of heart,
a solitary journey with the nine portals of a true beginning.
Silence sings in the country of banners and lively streams;
words should not be spoken in the time of Revelation.

Morning glory is only for those who have a heart.
The divine fire contains the dust of cosmic reality.
Stand firm, initiates, in the morning of Our new chart.
Our Fire is burning the remains of your opacity.
Your ardent fire is needed in this time of OM.
Prepare the goblet of fire and your sword,
the rising of Sirius is nearer to your home,
its intense blue is washing away the unwanted words.
Work hard to calm your fiery nature of old:
Our divine needs are sowing the seeds of the new world.

Our Temple is hidden in the heart of a diamond.
Its fifty six facets represent all aspects of Love.
The precious stones of Earth are the tears of the season.
Know the true path of Light and the one of the Dove.
At the gate of the new beginning
the anchor of Faith is still laying dormant
for those who have to strive towards Our coming.
Initiates! Guard well the gate of the Adamant.

Dive into the river of Om and prayers
Feel the power of the Word in your heart
Cleanse your body layers upon layers
And be ready to grasp the way of art.
For the Sun of the suns to raise upon the horizon
you need to stand on the cliff of dawn.
Bear the chalice of Our heart to the mount
And release Beauty within the pages of Wisdom.
Rare are those initiates who persevere and grow
as Our mount is rising only when you can see and bow.

The scent of your Flower spirals round your inner fire;
Give time to your progress for a swift evolution.
Set a time for a deep connection with Our pyre
And be ready for our requested direction.
Our time orbits around the nadis of Hierarchy and its Fire
Your most earnest striving always reaches Our attention.
Ban harmful thoughts! Their smell drives Us away.
Keep smiling even in the pale hour of initiation.
Our star will show its cosmic radiance in your newest day.

Remember: the reward is in the giving!

OM!

To me...

O Daughter of Mine!
Take the pen of reasoning and humility.
Raise your vibrations to the field of achievement.
Express closely your dependability
and assume simply the unfolding event.
Your heart shows its petals and its centre;
this has led you to climb the mountain of initiation.
Take the last steps close to the ridge and persevere
The fire awaits you at the door of immolation.
Soothing is the breeze of the north for the ardent.
Give your heart to the awakening.
The mandala of your soul shines in the betterment.
Your Brother of Old is ready for your becoming.

OM!

The pearls of Wisdom are hidden in Sirius

The blue will deepen with Faith and Concentration.

Remain firm while speaking about the Divine Syllabus.

The Flowers will have lost their petals before the Revelation.

Our banner has been placed on the mountain.
Look at the east and nowhere else.
A song needs to be heard from the plain
as Our warriors ride the steeds of the Earth.

Prepare your heart to encompass all aspects of Love.
Ripe is your fire in the midst of dawn.
Forget the cumbersome tasks of the world
and focus on the parchment of the Father and the Son.

The time of prayers is overshadowed by Our whirlwind;
Now have faith! Rise above the altar of the morning Sun.
No time is lost in the juvenile time of your becoming.
Gather under our banner and join the Sons of the Sun!

OM!

The Fire is on the altar
The three rays have mingled.
From them, the chalice is not afar
and the water of Life is being held.

Rule out the space of time
The temple has only one door.
The Father is singing the rhyme
for the Four to be the anchor.

OM!   OM!   OM!

All seeds germinate with the heat of the Sun
and the tender and loving care of the gardener;
The same for your thoughts while you run,
They weave your present and your future in a prayer.

Hierarchy was born out of the Light of the path.
All Bodhisattvas strove along this path with fortitude.
You will endure and gain victory over the past.
The blade of the sunlight will light up your gratitude.

OM!   OM!   OM!

The wheel of Life is an instrument of glory;
steer the wheel so as to show its radiance.
The stars have closed the bridge of rivalry
For unity is the only vessel linked up with transcendence.

Retrieve the memories of good and bounty.
The Lord of the three has risen from silence.
Our flowers will bloom for eternity
We inlaid their scent within the divine Presence.

Concentrate your colour on your inner diamond.
Its beam will echo with the sound of Shambhala.
In the Hierarchy the colours of your beam are paramount
As We use them for all Our stanzas.

In the deep well of your silence
We give you all instructions.
Be a divine vigil in this period of radiance.
We have thought of you and prepare the mount.

OM!   OM!   OM!

In the light blue Being embrace,
Sit like a child;
The cosmic landscape has changed its horizon.
Bring to your heart the colours of the rivers of delight
and carry Our banners on which Our heart is reason.
Review the conditions of the devic values
None has stained the purity of Hope
The highest Devas guide the fire of your psalms
and protect the colours of Our divine Abode.

The Mother of the World

Children of Love,
Keep your hearts filled with the sunlight of peace.
Our seas of colours govern the landscape of tomorrow.
Where lilies and roses grow and give their scent,
the Light of Love shines like a rainbow after the storm.
Pure is the one who keeps his thoughts on the highest waves.
My devas surf with him in synchronicity singing My mantra
Ride your unicorns with the Highest Ones on the
crest of dawn.
Sow Beauty again and again.
Follow our command through and through.
Our lotus will always bloom in the garden of your heart.

The mantle of Peace has yet to be worn by a human being
The Love of the Logos surrounds the World without
and within.
Sit across the east and bear the heat and the striving
as Our steeds of Light will need to ride above your rising.

OM!

To all Initiates...

The Fire has entered the house of the Lord.
Spirit can awaken in the land of the many.
Truth is only revealed in the geometry of the Word
Initiates! Be aware of the Messenger of the Hierarchy.

On the way to the mountains, the bridge has to be crossed
as the river is swollen after the cries of Humanity.
Each of you is carrying the joy and the burden of the cross
but Our hand is pushing you through austerity.

Evolution is the movement of infinite Love.
The Word of the Father has transcended His ideas.
Read the books of Light and those of the Dove.
The morning sun is brightening the garden of the
three Buddhas.

OM!   OM!   OM!

The key to enlightenment rests upon Our choosing.
The blue Sun of Our Presence illuminates all your centres
The chalice of eternity will assist you in this birthing
and the eternal fire will burn the resilient cinders.
Upon the altar of our inner chanting burns the ardent
Sun of the Father
His all Seeing Eye blazing the fiery hearts of all, shines
in the splendour of all-knowing.
Beware of His fire: you are heading to the furnace
of His prayer.
The Sirian Lord is waiting on the threshold of Orion
His cosmic arena is ready for the soaring of Time.
Wear the shield of transformation
Our ray will radiate upon your inner shrine.

In the exquisite clarity of the day
the soul has risen to the temple of gold;
the petals of her heart are afire with the ray,
at the gate of Ascension, stands the Lord of Old.
The strength of the spirit will grow and grow
as harmony lays the path with the pearls of Light.
Remember the nature of the flower and bow
whilst your soul serve Us with delight.
Strong is the will of the server
but caring are his thoughts and words.
In the antechamber of Our path and Sphere
Your vessels are filled with the Spirit of the Lords.

The bridge of Love has raised your ultimate goal.
The crucifixion happens only on the diamonds
of your centres.
Pay heed. Love always wins over the illusion of glory
and its call.
Blessed is the happiness of those living in the embrace
of Love's power.
If Wisdom were the Queen over all ranks of Humanity,
Peace would spring under the step of each human being.
Then the flowers of Our garden would be seen
in their divinity
sowing their seeds in the furrows of becoming.
Action is called for initiations and their mastery.
The road to victory is also like a flower in the morning sun.
Your battle is the one which leads to Harmony
even through the repeat of Beauty and its ardent Sun.

OM!

The roses of the temple will be eternally white
as nothing could change their Grace and Beauty.
Bring them the water of your Love and Purity
so they could keep the youth of My heart as a knight.

You are the guardians of an inestimable treasure;
face this Truth in the sanctuary of your heart.
Pull out all undesirable thoughts and displeasure
and your purest vibrations will soon reach Our Soul
and Heart.

In the kingdom of Our hearts we hold the eternal
Truth of being.
Enter its garden of mansuetude and infinite Light.
The towers of Shambhala will show you the seeds of striving
then your Flowers will truthfully blossom in Our Might.

OM!   OM!   OM!

For my birthday... text inspired by a Beloved Master...

The road to me has many avenues where trees grow like
brothers in the kingdom of Love.
Have you counted your blessings at the threshold of
your new beginning?
I sing for you the song of silence where wisdom is born
in a pool of stars.
Your consciousness is heightened in a stretch of infinite Light
and unfolds its wings in the cradle of Love.
Walk on the bridge of unity and steadfastness;
the pearls of Knowledge are glittering in the waters
of Happiness.
In the blue diamond of My Presence reside the devas
of the book of Time
writing the music of the future.
The mountain top has never been so near, its golden crown
bathing in a thousand sunsets.
On the path to its glory, I am the beggar of the stream,
the windsurfer of the slopes.
We shall meet at the early hour of Peace when the bells ring
the release of Time.
Be at the ready on the threshold of My heart: the star of the
North will reveal its splendour.

Our thread of Love is always guiding the initiate to
the mountain
but the pitfalls are plenty for whom doesn't accept fully
our Teachings.
Light prevails and curves your desire towards the goal
of the Fountain.
Strive on the rocky path on which the blades of grass sing.

Vigilance and extreme awareness are required in My domain.
Nothing will happen until you master Our singing.
You are Our warriors and shall not turn away from the pain.
With faith, all wounds should heal and unfold your wings.

We have given you the pure task for the new Dawn.
Wear the garment of Our school and the hat of Fire.
Think carefully about the future as knowledge is your crown.
In your hat We have poured the liquor of Our Power.

OM!   OM!   OM!

To me... and others!

I restored for you the echo chamber of Shambhala
Gratitude and Bliss resonate anew in its chambers.
You have to take the robe of the mountain and mandala
and pursue the traces of Light left by the Father.

The rigour of Teachings enliven your soul and mind
as the lilies and roses grow in the garden of delight and gates.
Holy words will enter your flaming heart and mind
to rinse away the vicissitudes of late.

The Laws have to be learned from the heart striving.
The Ones who progress and learn receive the lightnings
of My Power.
Enter My Abode at the threshold of the becoming
and I shall give you the chalice of My Flower.

OM!

The realm of the Child is not for the beginner.
Preparation is of importance and enacted by Love.
Without the heart no action is empowered.
Action! Action! Action! for the sake of Love.

then, vision of four sisters each carrying two buckets of salt...

Samskaras are the battle of the wise;
on their field the heart is unshelled and raw.
The gate will open on the hour of the rise
and reveal the splendour of the Law.
The arcana of the east should be made clearer
and remember the eight in the Mind exploration.
Pour the water of bliss in the name of the Father
and enter the gate which leads to initiation.

The heart of the matter is in the perception;
open your heart to its petals of gold.
There, is revealed the cradle of the bastion
built by the Brothers of Old.

The Serpent of Wisdom is raising its head
as its body of work girdles the realm of God.
In the sacred book of the Original Bread
It has written the words with the ink of Gold.

The source of your thoughts has to be divine.
The altar of tomorrow depends on its essence.
Reap the fruits which grow on the tree of Thine,
their flesh contains the blood of the Presence.

True are the initiates who silently bear hardship;
their Shield will be stronger and more refined.
It is on its cinders that the true Mind is built
where the Soul finds the cloak of Beauty defined.

OM!   OM!   OM!

The triune of our Light has empowered the Seven.
The well is dug in the field of plenty.
Let thy heart ascend to the blue omen
The pearls of your tears draw the sign of infinity.

When the Three and the Seven work together,
the Ten brings His casket of gold,
and claiming the era of the Divine Father
raises the banner of the Battle of Old.

Ô Daughters of our old school of Light,
Wear the Three and the Seven in your heart
Bearing Our Names as Our Shield of Might.

OM!   OM!   OM!

To me... and the many Sisters and Brothers...

Apply the rules you have learned since eons.
The cosmic rules are laid by the Lord of the Lords.
You have to treasure them for your evolution
and learn to love their realm as a warrior.

Walk through Our Garden with the smile of an initiate,
The songs of victory have never been so close.
Amidst Our flowers, you will find the lily of the seven gates.
Breathe its perfume to face the chalice of the Rose.

Surrender to the golden voice of your Brother of Old
and lay naked in front of His Song of Might.
A new robe is waiting in the antechamber of Gold
and it shall reveal the purity of your Light.

Do not forget the song of the mountains,
the note of destiny is hidden in its core of bliss.
Keep silence in this hour of ordain,
your dragon of fire has carried you over the Precipice.

The steps of Our march are counted.
The mountains are covered with snow.
We shall leave footprints for the prepared
as Our hands wave those We bestow.

Ripples spread on the waters of knowledge
Assert more your knowing and you shall conquer.
The world is waiting for your pledge;
We are listening to the song of your power.

The Ancient of Days has raised His finger.
The road has been cleared of ignorance.
Straightforward is the path to the Father
where the fires of His divine Wisdom dance.

The Service is received by the enlightened Ones
Bear the weight of the immolation
The Teacher has entrusted the exalted Ones
On the mountain path happens all manifestation.

A rose cannot be cut without knowing its heart.
Let Light pour on the body of the Becoming.
Your mind should be set on the highest learning
in manifesting actions on the fire of Our Heart.

Your purposeful battles have only one aim: Beauty
Remain centred in the alleys of wonderment.
At the appointed time, the realisation will land in Harmony.
Service! Service! Service! Aim at Enlightenment!

To me... and all Sisters and Brothers!

All ways and paths are travelled through and through.
The Light of your soul lies transformed before Us
as the path of Destiny has restored your Trust.
The veil is lifted. You can "see" all through and through.
Regain your balance in your striving to serve.
Your heartland has never been so aflame.
Therefore guard the gate of the Teaching of the Verb;
With Beauty and Love the chalice of initiation is shielded.

The Tribes of Heaven are descending on an ardent Fire;
Each of Them holds a golden coin of the Heart Centre.
Their vision of peace resembles your soul in the cradle
of the Father.
In a misty dawn a perfect hour is being born out
of the Divine Mother.

The colours of Our banners have been washed and
are now more visible.
Raise your hands to receive the water of purification.
The Brotherhood has read the signs on a page of the Bible.
Be at the ready! We shall lead you to the arduous road
of initiation.

OM!   OM!   OM!

I have sown the seed of Love in your morning garment.
I raised the banner of the seven to energise your Harmony.
I poured the nectar of Light in the chalice of the present.
And gave you the song of the three in the sunrise of Destiny.

Bear the weight of solitude but keep your heart in Grace.
The mentor of the hills has to draw the lines
of his limitations.
Keep high the aim of your Soul Purpose and raise.
Our Brotherhood recites Its mantra and beams Its
divine vibrations.

Challenging events at times are necessary
as they reveal the hidden side of Self.
Truth has to brighten your skies and intimacy
to offer you the strength of the Higher Self.

Pleading has never helped those united as a All.
Free-will is Our law and its strict acceptance
is the first mandate of Our Chart wall.
Our Love has neither frontier nor dependence.

Restore the balance of your divine unfoldment
Our Path has its mountains and valleys.
Initiation is not without loss and bereavement
so as to cleanse the diamond of your Rays.

You are not starting a battle
but a path of forgiveness and prayer.
See always the best on Our divine table
The Wheel of Destiny has only One Father.

OM!   OM!   OM!

From Guru Rimpoché...

Impressions are for the heart not the Mind.
Constantly follow what your heart is showing
You shall always find me on the Light behind
See your heart filled with Beauty: it will start burning!

The lotus on the lake shows the path of the Heart.
Within the centre of the flower blooms My Love.
I have hidden its Light not to blind your start.
On the wings of Hope, dive into My lake of Love.

OM AH HUNG VAJRA GURU PADMA SIDDHI HUNG

To me... after a special ceremony

The pearls of destiny are on the necklace of dawn.
Open your heart to the fire of the Sun.
One by one the pearls shine with what you have sown.
The Ancient of Days embeds His finger in your Sun.
At the golden gate place your forehead on the Door;
The imprint of Light will radiate its splendour
and becomes the key of the flight that soar.
Release all attachment and become one with My rigour.

OM!

O Beloved disciples, children of My Heart
Testings can be hard to bear but are necessary.
A diamond cannot shine without friction and the
cleansing of infinity.
Each of you is a diamond for Our divine school of Heart.

Bring your sword of Light to the fore
And raise it above Our altar of Love.
The sparkles of Wisdom will be inlaid to the core
as We sing the mantra of the House of the Dove.

OM!

Ô Children of Mine!

The Three empower you with the Five
The purbas of Light are raised to Our Home
Link them with the OM of Our Brothers who thrive
As their stars will alight your temple at dawn.

Storms are battering the Humanity of All.
Rain has to cleanse the ancient ways of being.
Keep your sword of Love raised to Our Great Hall
And Our words will grace your Becoming.

Rivers are born from a trickle of Light
But nothing stops them fertilising all land.
Rivers of Love have their source in the Sun Light.
Bring Our Presence even in the hearts of sand.

OM!   OM!   OM!

Ô Daughter of Mine!

You must wear the cloak of serenity
before entering the sanctuary of the Bride.
Resume the palpable effort of sanctity
as the golden crown of Love is becoming your ride.

Bring the tool of meditation to the level of the Rose
then I shall dive My divine sword in your heart.
Your blood will run into Mine in the river that arose
The divine union of purpose will be etched in My heart.

OM!   OM!   OM!

Repose upon My heart when life is shaking your being
The way of the heart is sown in purity and sanctity.
Nothing can lead you better than the act of yielding
as it is where Our Temple of Truth is clothed in Beauty.

The Arch is ablaze with Our cosmic rays
Under the canopy of Our divine Wisdom.
It is Our plan you are bringing on radiant Ways!
Check the details of it through the sound of Om.

Rise to the kingdom of Our spiritual Land.
The brilliant star of Sirius will lead you there
as the Teaching will empower your Wand
to reveal the true power of the Divine Mother.

The temple of old is to strive for victory!
Be vigilant and work under Our banner.
The road to Truth is paved with bravery;
As its warriors, your battle is aglow with Fire.

OM!

To me...

The Lords of Time have built your soul gate
Its dome of Light has received its golden garment.
The Master stands radiant in prayer and waits:
Your hour has come from the depth of attainment.

The gate of faith has risen to the Eye.
You have passed winter with the scent of spring.
Gather the banners under Our watchful Eye;
It is time we start afresh with Our Teaching.

The auric colours need to be appraised and cleansed.
Our names will vibrate but are very demanding!
Source the Light from the dome of Shambhalic beams;
Nothing will hinder the splendour of Our Blessing.

Strive within to reach the intense quietude of meditation.
Erect soundly the temple of Contemplation and Beauty.
The lightning of Our words will brighten the ascension.
The Divine Sower shall bless your unfailing constancy.

OM!   OM!   OM!

A special message...

Bring your medicant bowl
and I will give you a grain of rice.
Bring the candles of the heart of All
and I shall pour the nectar of the wise.

Battle only with your sword of Love,
its blade has the Sun inlaid within.
Don't be afraid to stand all alone
as the power of your love is what We use therein.

Recite the holy names who gather in your heart centre
Give them the best of each of your wings.
Assent to the law of giving and surrender
My Temple lives within your golden dawning.

The combat, "O warriors of mine", is of Love.
The power to act is given by My Brother.
The essence is spread under the house of the Dove
Your Brothers of Old guide you under Their Banner.

Upon the high peaks of the mountain of revelation
the eagle has soared to the divine kingdom.
The Eye of the Ancient of Days sees your communion.
Nothing can stop your ascension to Our OM.

The finest and hardest of all battles still stand within.
as We want you to wear the golden dress of the east.
Hearken! Sons and Daughters of the new Beginning
The sound of Shambhala announces the death of the Beast.

OM!   OM!   OM!

You are harbingers of cosmic Light
and nothing will stop the flares of Its rays.
Soar to the plain of Shambhalic Might,
the heralds of dawn will sing Our Ways.

The Divine Mother cannot yet show Her radiant face.
The Feminine Principle is to be understood.
She bore the radiant children of the human race
and is the dawning of Our Holy Brotherhood.

The cosmic wings will soon unfold their mighty Presence
to unveil the ascending road to your true Mind.
Be aware of Our Teaching and the Fire of its stance
with it, your wings will enliven Our cosmic Mind.

All hardships are illusionary.
They are your resistance to change and grow.
Ban all fear and any bigotry.
Uplift your gaze and see the seed to sow.

Major changes are filling the current dawn.
Your participation is required fully.
Always remember how you have been warned:
by Our Mind impregnating yours ceaselessly.

The Divine Mother has lifted Her gaze
and radiates Her presence upon your soul.
Between Her hands is the Light of the Sage.
At Her feet, bow the stars and their soul.

To me...

The patient hour has its reward
Turn your gaze towards the star.
Be vigilant, true but on your guard
Pure consciousness is awakening your altar.

Do not turn away from predestined time
Hours have wings but also fire
The song of Wisdom has given you a rhyme
to pour Love on your heart pyre.

The source of Life comes from different mountains
Climb on the one which is a Blue Light
The Cross of Shambhala is not there in vain
All initiates should stand close to its Might.

Revere the integrated mandala of Love
Each colour is inserted like a spiritual jewel.
Deepen your connection with the dove
The miracle of faith is unveiling its golden bell.

The symbols have given their geometry and sound.
Their music inhabits the shaft of your soul and spirit.
Your sword of Light is wielded high from the ground,
   its geometry of Love bound to the Master's visit.

Ride the fiery steed of the Faithful cavalry.
The mantle of Truth is wrapped on your shoulders.
The glorious Sun has risen upon the Hierarchy
Its open gate shows the hand of the Divine Sower.

OM!   OM!   OM!

The gate of purity has freed its flow of Light
showing its intensity on your body of glory.
Let pure thoughts be a glorious sight
and raise your gaze to contemplate the Almighty.

The very name of the Master is your shield
as He pours His Blessings on the radiance of your destiny.
Be at the divine task and strive and yield.
There is no other path to Truth than Serenity.

OM!

To T.

The Robe of the monk has to be cleansed in layers.
His body of Light is tuned to the school of Wisdom.
The Lord has asked for more discipline and prayers
so as to pay heed and yield to the sound of OM.
The waters have been released from the fountain of Love.
The lake shimmers in the sunrise of the mount.
Deepen, deepen your silence under the wings of the Dove,
Humbleness and strength are for the Initiate without doubt.

O Daughter of Mine!

The seeds of the river of Love are holding tight
opening their heads to the purest sunrise.
Your spiritual Desire is dynamised by Our Might.
The cosmic Visitors will be announced by surprise.

The crossing of the bridge is not taken without caution
as changes are coming in the high ranks of Humanity.
Attunement will be needed at all times and seasons.
Wisdom and Love are the most potent songs for Unity.

OM!

Like one unified heart
See the rise of your swords of Light.
Your hearts in Our Hearts
Feel the power of Our Might.

In the leaves of your inner garden
We wrote the Wisdom of the ages,
Your tree of life has been laden
with the wondrous words of the Sages.

Stand firm amidst the ires of Tomorrow,
your flaming hearts united as one.
Serene are your souls on Our Rainbow
Initiates! Sing the Song of the One.

OM!   OM!   OM!

BIOGRAPHY

After studying, immersing herself in Philosophy and some of the world's Spiritual Philosophies and their Wisdoms, including Psychology, Energetic Anthropology, (J.T. Zeberio) and Esoteric Studies, Eliane moved to Scotland more than thirty years ago. Here she has been pursuing her own research on the purpose of Life and Evolution with the strong presence of her Love for God, the Source of All of Life, and, not least, through her inner spiritual journey.

Having in her heart and soul this constant inner Source of Light which fills her with Joy and Serenity, she received in meditation inspirational guidance and lyrical poetry which she diligently transcribed on her notepads. This book is the result of these deep meditations, even contemplations, where the Divine Light has infused the pages with Harmony and Beauty.

Eliane presently gives spiritual teachings and guidance helping probationers and disciples to better discover their Soul Mission and the ineffable ways of the Masters of the Spiritual Hierarchy.

Lightning Source UK Ltd.
Milton Keynes UK
UKHW022022230921
391093UK00006B/196